Essentials of Annuities

Steven M. Bragg

AccountingTools®

ISBN 978-1-64221-169-6

For more information about AccountingTools® products, visit our Web site at www.accountingtools.com.

Table of Contents

About the Author

Steven Bragg, CPA, has been the chief financial officer or controller of four companies, as well as a consulting manager at Ernst & Young. He received a master's degree in finance from Bentley College, an MBA from Babson College, and a Bachelor's degree in Economics from the University of Maine. He has been a two-time president of the Colorado Mountain Club, and is an avid alpine skier, mountain biker, and certified master diver. Mr. Bragg resides in Centennial, Colorado. He has written more than 300 books and courses, including *New Controller Guidebook*, *GAAP Guidebook*, and *Payroll Management*.

Steven maintains the accountingtools.com web site, which contains continuing professional education courses, the Accounting Best Practices podcast, and thousands of articles on accounting subjects.

Buy Additional AccountingTools Courses

AccountingTools offers more than 1,500 hours of CPE courses, with concentrations in accounting, auditing, finance, taxation, and ethics. Related courses that you might like include:

- Essentials of Life Insurance
- Estate Planning Fundamentals
- Investing Guidebook
- Wealth Management

Go to accountingtools.com/cpe to view these additional courses.

AccountingTools®

Essentials of Annuities

Introduction

An *annuity* is a series of fixed payments made at regular intervals. It has a number of uses, of which the primary one is to fund a person's retirement. As such, it is intended to be a supplement to a person's social security payments. In addition, it is a mechanism for deferring the payment of income taxes on any gains experienced.

The returns from an annuity are the result of an agreement under which the recipient originally paid a sum to an insurer, with the institution pledging to return the funds at a later date, plus interest. The payment phase during which the investment fund is built up is called the *accumulation phase*, while the payment phase during which annuity payments are made is called the *annuitization phase*. The accumulation phase may consist of a single payment, or it may involve a series of payments over a long period of time. The annuitization phase is not entirely clear-cut. You might opt for a continuing series of payments, or you might park the cash in the annuity product permanently, with the intent of forwarding it to a beneficiary once you die. In short, the timing and amounts of the cash inflows to and outflows from an annuity product can vary substantially.

Risks Covered by Annuities

Why purchase an annuity contract? You are probably concerned about various types of risks that might arise during the remainder of your life. One of these risks is *longevity risk*, which is the risk that you will outlive your retirement savings. There are income annuity products that guard against this risk by guaranteeing periodic payouts, no matter how long you live. Another risk is *investment risk*, which is the potential for you to experience a loss on an investment. This loss may come from a market decline, an increased rate of inflation, the bankruptcy of a securities issuer, and so forth. This is a particular concern for those people approaching or in retirement, who cannot afford to suffer losses on their accumulated funds. There are deferred annuity products that guard against this risk by guaranteeing a certain amount of income, which in some cases may even be indexed for inflation.

There is also the risk of overspending. This might be due to being a (relatively) young retiree who now has the time to travel, and so spends an inordinate amount of money. It might also be due to monetary gifts to children, who routinely appear to have pressing needs. It might also be due to a simple loss of interest in finances as you get older, which can result in a certain amount of overspending. These issues can be addressed by an income annuity, which guarantees that you will always have access to a certain payout amount, month after month, no matter what else happens.

Examples of Annuity Scenarios

Under what scenarios would it make sense to enter into an annuity contract? The following three scenarios are representative of situations that might call for an annuity:

Scenario 1

David is 75 years old, and wants to be certain of having sufficient income to pay for his expenses until he dies. To do so, he pays a lump sum to an insurer, which commits to provide him with a basic level of income starting at age 80, and continuing through his death, no matter how far off in the future that may be.

Scenario 2

Amanda will need $50,000 in ten years to pay for her granddaughter's first year of college. She is unwilling to take the chance that investing her current savings in the stock market might result in losses. So, she purchases an annuity contract that guarantees a minimum 4% rate of return for the next ten years, at which point she will have the $50,000 that she needs.

Scenario 3

Allen is a big saver. He has already invested the maximum amount in an individual retirement account, and in a simplified employee pension plan. He still has money left over, and wants to invest it in a tax-deferred saving vehicle. Accordingly, he puts the excess cash into an annuity. He is not concerned about the value of the funds in the annuity fluctuating over time, he just wants to make sure that any earnings generated are tax-deferred.

A different annuity type would apply to each of these scenarios. The main point is that a broad range of annuity products are available that can address nearly any investment scenario that you might devise. This brings up the question of why people buy annuities. The preceding scenarios offer some clues, but the main reasons are as follows:

- *Charitable giving*. An annuity can be designed to pay you a reasonable amount in retirement, and then pay out any remaining funds at your death to a favored charity. There are several variations on the concept.
- *Earnings protection*. Some types of annuities provide guaranteed earnings. This is especially useful when you absolutely, positively need to earn a certain amount from an initial investment, usually in order to make a fixed payment as of a future date. Furthermore, these annuities provide peace of mind to those people who cannot afford to take a loss on their investments – such as those approaching retirement.
- *Pay for medical expenses*. End-of-life care is very expensive, so there are annuity products that can be used to pay for it. These annuities allow a person to accelerate payouts to deal with these expenses.

- *Retirement income.* Some types of annuities are structured to pay out during your retirement, possibly through the end of your life. Thus, an annuity represents a form of supplemental retirement income, on top of your social security payments.
- *Tax-deferred income.* A major reason to purchase an annuity contract is to take advantage of its tax-deferred status. Wealthier people acquire annuities in order to avoid paying income taxes on their annual investment earnings. This avoidance compounds over time, resulting in substantial earnings. There is no cap on the amount you can invest in these annuities, making them a great choice for increasing your investment earnings over the long term.

The Main Annuity Products

The main types of annuity products are described in the following sub-sections. Each one can be structured as an immediate annuity or a deferred annuity. An *immediate annuity* provides an immediate guaranteed lifetime payout, typically in monthly or quarterly installments. The downside to this option is that you are trading away the initial lump-sum payment for the lifetime annuity. A *deferred annuity* provides a guaranteed lump sum or series of payments, which begin at some point in the future. This approach allows your principal to grow before any payouts occur. The payout stage can be quite deferred, resulting in a considerable accumulation of wealth.

Fixed Annuities

In a *fixed annuity*, you are handing over a chunk of money to an insurer (perhaps all at once, or with several ongoing payment requirements). The insurer pools the money with payments coming in from other individuals and then invests it in safe government securities and corporate bonds. In the unlikely event that one of these issuers defaults, the insurer is liable for the loss, not you. This reduces your risk of loss, though not entirely – there is a chance that the insurer will go bankrupt.

Fixed annuities are set with specific payout dates, such as a full payout in five years, or ten years. This is a good choice when the goal is to grow a sum of money for a specific period of time, and especially when you need a targeted amount of cash at the end of that time.

A fixed annuity is a low-risk option, and is likely to generate a higher rate of return than a certificate of deposit, though not as high as an index fund. The insurer may guarantee a minimum rate of return, though this may only be for the first year of the contract. Also, any gains experienced are tax-deferred, while returns are compounded over time. A further advantage is that you may be able to take partial withdrawals from the invested funds over the term of the annuity contract.

The main types of fixed annuities are as follows:

- *Single-year guaranteed fixed annuity.* In this contract, the rate of return is guaranteed for the first year, after which it can vary. This first-year rate may be an unusually high teaser rate, in which case you can reasonably assume that the rate of return will decline thereafter.

- *Fixed indexed annuity*. Its yield is linked to the movement of a specific market index. Under this contract, the insurer purchases options on how a market index will perform. If the market index improves during the option period, the insurer exercises the option and locks in the index gain. If the index goes down instead, then the option is not exercised, resulting in no gain. In short, you may experience a gain or no gain, but you will not experience a loss. The main contract options in these agreements are as follows:

  o *Choose a market index*. Select the market index on which you want the insurer to purchase options. Examples are the S&P 500 index and the Russell 2000 index. You can pick a combination of indexes.
  o *Choose a reset period*. It is customary to pick a one-year reset period, which is when any interest gains are credited to your account.
  o *Choose a term length*. A 10-year length is sufficiently long to protect you from any market crashes prior to your retirement. Or, choose some other duration if you are targeting needing the money as of a specific date.

  A concern with fixed indexed annuities is that you are not paid the full amount of the gain when an index increases; this is because the gain is actually derived from a pair of options that only capture a portion of the gain. The result can be relatively low returns.

- *Multi-year guaranteed annuity*. In this contract, the rate of return is guaranteed for the life of the contract. This contract provides a high degree of predictability, since the rate is guaranteed.

Variable Annuities

A variable annuity focuses on increasing the return to the investor. It does so by investing in securities that generate higher returns, but which also have a greater risk of loss. The point is not to generate an ongoing income stream for the investor, so it does not distribute any gains, interest, or dividends – instead, everything is re-invested. And, since these funds are tax-deferred, investors can put off the related tax bill for quite a long time.

Variable annuities are a good investment option for wealthier investors who are searching for higher rates of return, like to shift their investments among different funds, and who are willing to take on a certain amount of risk. Furthermore, these investors may never need the cash at all, in which case their beneficiaries will inherit the contracts.

A particular benefit of variable annuities is that your invested funds are safe from creditors if the insurer goes bankrupt. This is a key advantage over purchasing a fixed annuity, where your funds are at risk of loss if the insurer goes under.

> **Tip:** Variable annuities can be complicated financial products, so be sure to ask for and peruse any hypothetical examples of how a proposed annuity would perform under certain circumstances.

There are a number of variable annuity features to be aware of. The key features are as follows:

- *Annuitization option.* You have the option to convert the deferred payout on the contract to a series of regularly-scheduled payments.
- *Death benefits.* The contract will at least pay beneficiaries the cash value of the contract at your death, though options are available that will pay an increased death benefit – for a fee, of course.
- *Investment options.* You will have the option to invest your funds in a variety of sub-accounts, each of which is structured as a different type of mutual fund, with different risk and return characteristics.
- *Surrender period.* The contract will limit the amount of funds that you can withdraw from the annuity for a number of years. This feature is required, so that the insurer will have sufficient funds on hand from which to recover the commission that it paid your agent.

The main types of fixed annuities are as follows:

- *Investment-only variable annuities.* This is a low-fee annuity that is intended for people who have already maxed out their IRA and 401(k) investments, and want to park more money in an investment vehicle that offers tax-deferred returns.
- *Variable annuities with a guaranteed lifetime withdrawal benefit.* This annuity is used to lock down a specific amount of guaranteed income for the rest of your life, while also giving you the right to withdraw funds from the account at any time. This is a highly flexible annuity with many options, but the downside is that the associated commissions and fees can be quite high. Also, these can be confusing contracts, and so should only be entered into after consulting with a knowledgeable advisor.

Income Annuities

An *income annuity* is similar to a pension plan, because it generates a stream of income payments that will fund your retirement. This can be a good choice for someone who is concerned about not having sufficient cash to provide a steady income through his or her later years.

A deferred income annuity is intended to start returning cash later in a person's retirement. This annuity costs less, since it has a later payout date, and ensures that you will not outlive your savings. A variation on the concept is the medically-underwritten income annuity, which is designed for people with life threatening conditions. Following an examination, the insurer will assess your likely lifespan and offer a lower-cost annuity, on the grounds that you are more likely to die at an earlier age than the average person, and so will receive fewer periodic payments.

A particular advantage of an income annuity is that it provides you with the security of a guaranteed stream of income payments, which may be no small matter when you have few other sources of reliable ongoing payments (such as a pension). Furthermore, with this income guaranteed, you might be more inclined to invest the remainder of your savings in riskier investments that may provide a greater return. In effect, an income annuity may increase your risk tolerance.

Income annuities also have disadvantages, one of which is that these contracts contain a significant insurance component. As is the case with any insurance policy, there are winners (those who live longer) and there are losers (those who do not). If you die earlier than expected, then you lose, and some portion (or all) of your remaining invested funds will be used to make payments to those who live longer than you. Another issue is that your funds will be locked away and inaccessible; this is the trade-off you make when you agree to the series of income payments that the insurer makes back to you.

There are two main types of income annuities, which are as follows:

- *Immediate income annuity*. Under this arrangement, you pay a lump sum at retirement, and the insurer pays you a regular income for the rest of your life. Each individual payment made by the insurer is lower than the payments made under the deferred income annuity (as described next), because the deferred option allows your investment earnings to build up for a longer period of time before payments begin.
- *Deferred income annuity*. Under this arrangement, you schedule when you want to start receiving periodic payments from the insurer. The longer you wait, the lower the price of the contract.

For either of these income annuity types, you can specify that it be a *lifetime* income annuity (where you are paid until you die) or a *period certain income annuity*, where you are only paid for a fixed period of time. Also for either annuity type, you will receive a larger payment if you begin the contract sooner, so that the funds can be invested and earn a return for a longer period of time.

You can also specify whether the annuity be set up as a single-life policy or a joint and survivor annuity. Under a single-life arrangement, you personally will receive payments for the rest of your life; this approach results in relatively large periodic payments. Or, under the joint and survivor arrangement, payments will be made for as long as you or your spouse remain alive. Since the joint and survivor arrangement will likely run for a longer period of time than the single-life arrangement, the periodic payments under a joint and survivor contract will be somewhat smaller.

> **Tip:** It can make sense to structure a joint and survivor income annuity to reduce the payments made to the surviving spouse. Doing so increases payments when both parties are alive; reduced payments for the survivor may be tenable, since there are fewer living expenses for one person.

Qualified and Non-Qualified Annuities

There are also qualified and non-qualified annuities. A *qualified annuity* is purchased with funds that are in a tax-deductible traditional individual retirement account, or an employer-sponsored retirement plan. You are required to take a required minimum distribution from these accounts once you reach age 73, which will be taxable. Conversely, a *non-qualified annuity* is acquired with savings on which you have already paid income tax. For these annuities, there is no requirement to take required minimum distributions from them; income tax is only owed if you elect to withdraw from them.

Reverse Mortgages

A *reverse mortgage* allows you to borrow against the equity stored up in your home, while still living in it. This loan can be taken as a lump sum, as a line of credit, or in the form of an annuity that pays out funds in regular installments over your life expectancy. This loan is not repaid until you eventually sell the home or die. When either event occurs, the house is sold, the reverse mortgage is paid off, and the remainder either goes to you (if you are still alive) or your beneficiary (if you are not). In the meantime, interest and fees are added to the loan balance each month, so that the loan balance continues to grow over time. However, the homeowner is required to pay property taxes and homeowners' insurance, and continue to live in the home.

The amount that you can borrow on a reverse mortgage is driven by the amount of equity you have in your home, as well as the applicable interest rate at the time when you take on the loan. A higher interest rate translates into a lower payout to you.

There are several major advantages to reverse mortgages. First, an older person now has the opportunity to continue living in his or her home, rather than being forced into cheaper accommodations. Second, the homeowner owes no taxes on the amount borrowed under a reverse mortgage arrangement. And finally, there is no need to pay down the mortgage until you sell the house, which may be a long ways off.

The main downside of a reverse mortgage is that it costs more than a traditional mortgage. A reverse mortgage includes charges for mortgage insurance, mortgage origination fees, other closing costs, and servicing fees. In addition, you may need to use some of the funds from a reverse mortgage to pay for the upkeep of your home, which may be a substantial amount for an older property. And finally, the amount of the loan that can be taken against your home may be relatively small, since the lender needs to recoup the value of not only the initial loan, but also the ongoing interest costs and other fees.

Annuities Involving Lifetime Income

Some annuity products commit to pay you for the rest of your life, no matter how long it may be. How can an insurance company do this? The secret is in the use of risk pooling. Under these arrangements, incoming funds are placed in a pool, from which investments are made. The insurer pays the contract owners from this pool for as long as they live. The insurer makes these payments from the investment returns of the fund, as well as from the original amounts contributed to the pool. In addition, payments are made from the funds left in the pool whenever any contract owner dies earlier than expected. Thus, you can "win" from this arrangement if you live longer than the other contract owners in the pool. If you die younger, then – in effect – you lose.

How to Acquire an Annuity

How do you acquire an annuity? The basic process is to first contact an insurer or a broker who represents that institution as an agent. The initial discussion covers your financial situation and what types of annuity products might work for you. Next, you complete an annuity application form, which is submitted to the insurer for approval. If the insurer approves of your application, then it sends you a final contract, which you have up to 30 days to review before signing and returning it. If you do so, then the insurer pays the broker a commission (which can be substantial) in exchange for processing the sale.

The Terms of an Annuity Contract

An annuity contract contains several key features of which you should be aware. The first point is that there are three parties involved in the contract. The first is the annuity *owner*, which is the person who signed the contract and pays all premiums. This may be one person, or a married couple or a trust that represents a person. The second party is the *annuitant*, who is the party that is entitled to receive annuity payments. This may be the owner, or someone else. The dates on which annuity payments occur is derived from the age of the annuitant. For example, Joe pays for an annuity contract, and is its owner. The annuitant is his daughter Mary, who is to receive lifetime income from it once she turns 65. The insurance company that is administering the contract will calculate the cost of the contract and the amount to be paid out based on Mary's life expectancy, not Joe's.

The third party to an annuity contract is the beneficiary. A *beneficiary* is the person who receives assets when someone else dies. A beneficiary is named in an annuity contract by the owner. The annuitant's beneficiary is also named. The owner and the annuitant can name each other as their beneficiaries, which is common for married couples.[1]

---

[1] The main choices for how a beneficiary can accept funds from an inherited annuity are to withdraw the funds in a lump sum, or to withdraw the funds over a period of up to five years.

An annuity contract contains several key clauses that you should be aware of. They are as follows:

- *Annuitization clause.* Annuitization is the process of converting the value of the investments in an annuity to a stream of income payments. This clause defines the duration of these payments, which may be for a specific time period, or for the rest of your or your spouse's life.

- *Death benefits clause.* In the event of the contract owner's death, the beneficiary receives a death benefit. This can be a substantial amount, depending on the nature of the benefit. It might, for example, be the amount of the original investment, or the value of those investments as of the death date, or even the highest value of the contract on any contract anniversary date.

- *Free-look periods clause.* The various state governments have mandated a period of time during which you can cancel a contract, which can be up to 30 days from the contract receipt date. This allows you a chance to consider whether you really want to enter into the contract, which may be a concern when you think an agent pushed you into the contract.

- *Inflation protection rider.* This rider requires the insurer to boost your payouts under an income annuity to keep pace with the inflation rate. Otherwise, your payments will likely have less purchasing power over time – which can be a major problem in a high-inflation environment. This can be an expensive option.

- *Long-term care option.* An annuity can contain an option (essentially insurance) that pays the cost of your long-term care, as long as you continue to pay an annual rider fee.

- *Market value adjusted (MVA) clause.* This clause imposes a penalty if you want to withdraw more funds than the contractually permitted amount. It is used by the insurer to keep you from shopping around elsewhere for better annuity contracts. The penalty is a combination of a surrender charge (as discussed shortly) and a downward adjustment in your account value.

- *Pass-through rate clause.* An annuity contract might allow you to earn the full amount of the interest earned by the insurer on your funds, minus a set percentage margin. This differs from the usual arrangement, where the insurer generates the best return it can on your funds, pays you a lower percentage, and keeps the difference. This arrangement can earn you a higher rate of return.

- *Payment type clause.* An income annuity typically requires a single up-front payment. If you want to obtain additional income from this type of contract, you will need to obtain a separate annuity contract. However, if you obtain a variable annuity, it may contain an option for you to make a number of additional payments over time.

The spouse of the deceased party also has the option to assume ownership of the contract and continue it.

- *Replacement annuity option.* This clause states whether the annuity is new, or being swapped for a pre-existing annuity. This can be an important issue, since a swap earns the agent another commission over the one already earned from the original annuity contract.
- *Single life with refund clause.* If you purchase a single life income annuity, insist on the single life with refund clause. This allows your beneficiaries to receive the remaining unused premium. Otherwise, once you die, no funds will be paid to your beneficiaries – even if you die soon after entering into the annuity contract.
- *Surrender periods clause.* A surrender period is the amount of time that the owner must wait before withdrawing any funds from an annuity without incurring a penalty. These periods can span a number of years, prior to which a surrender charge will be imposed. This period is required by the insurer, so that it can recover the cost of the commission paid to your agent.

> **Note:** No surrender period typically applies to withdrawals made to comply with your required minimum distribution – which the government requires to draw down your tax-protected retirement accounts after you reach a certain age (which is currently 73).

Annuity Fees

The types and amounts of fees charged will vary (a lot) by annuity contract, so we will not try to estimate the exact costs that you will incur. Instead, we will focus on the types of fees that you may be charged. They are as follows:

- *Contract fee.* This annual fee is set as a percentage of the amount invested in an annuity contract.
- *Investment fee.* This annual fee is charged for the investment options you select.
- *Surrender charge.* This is the fee you will be charged if you withdraw your money early.

There are also several types of fees that are only imposed on certain types of annuity contracts. For example:

- *Death benefit.* Upon payment of a fee, this rider creates a death benefit for a beneficiary.
- *Income rider.* Upon payment of a fee, this rider converts your invested funds into an income annuity; this is found in a variable annuity.

> **Note:** The fees associated with a fixed annuity are not stated in the contract. Instead, the insurer earns a profit from the difference between what it can earn from investing your assets and the rate of return that it has guaranteed to pay to you.

The fees associated with annuities can certainly pile up. These fees are needed by the insurer to pay commissions, market its products, make investments, hedge those investments, comply with government oversight, and more.

The Tax Impact of Annuities

Generally, and depending on the type of annuity product, an annuity is treated for tax purposes like an individual retirement account. This means that you pay no tax on any gains generated by the annuity until you remove funds from it.[2] However, if you withdraw funds before age 59½, you will incur a tax penalty[3]. Beyond these general concepts, the tax rules vary somewhat, depending on the circumstances. Here are the key issues:

- *Qualified annuities.* A common occurrence is for a person to have a large amount stored in a 401(k) retirement plan, which is then transferred into a rollover IRA once the person leaves the employer. The funds in this rollover account can then be dropped into a qualified annuity. Thereafter, any distributions from the qualified annuity will be taxed at the ordinary income tax rate. Many people invest in qualified annuities simply because they already have most of their money parked in an IRA.
- *Nonqualified annuities.* If you buy an annuity with after-tax dollars, then the taxes on any subsequent gains will be deferred. If the annuity is a deferred annuity (where you are not receiving periodic payments from it), then when you do decide to take a distribution, any accumulated gains must be withdrawn first – and taxed. After that, the principal can be withdrawn tax-free. However, if you instead purchased an income annuity, the rule about accumulated gains being withdrawn first does not apply. Instead, you use the exclusion ratio to spread out the tax obligation. The exclusion ratio is the percentage of your return that is not subject to taxes, and is calculated as a percentage of the return on your initial investment. Any return above the exclusion ratio is subject to taxes.

EXAMPLE

At Greg's retirement age of 65, he invests $200,000 in a single premium immediate annuity. In exchange, the insurer commits to pay $1,000 a month ($12,000 per year) for the rest of his life. According to life expectancy tables, Greg should live for another 20 years. Therefore, his expected return on the arrangement is $240,000 (20 years × $12,000).

---

[2] There is no penalty on income from an annuity as long as you don't withdraw funds before age 59½. Prior to that time, the IRS will charge a 10% penalty on each withdrawal.
[3] There are exceptions to the tax penalty for withdrawing funds before age 59½. It does not apply when the withdrawal is taken as an income annuity, or because you died, or the withdrawal was caused by your total, permanent disability.

Because Greg's initial $200,000 premium payment is 83.33 percent of the $240,000 expected return, he can exclude 83.33% of the $12,000 of annual annuity income from his taxable income. This means that he will only have to pay income tax on the remaining 16.66% of his income, which is $2,000.

Annuities are not a great method for passing wealth along to the next generation, since they will inherit the full amount of your tax liabilities, along with any funds given to them through an annuity product.

Advantages of Annuities

There are several advantages associated with annuity products, though the significance of these advantages will vary, depending on the annuity product in question. They are as follows:

- *Avoid probate court.* When you die, your assets and liabilities will likely go through probate court. This ties up your net assets for an extended period of time, while also incurring legal fees. Depending on the annuity contract, it can avoid probate and go straight to your beneficiaries, thereby sidestepping these irritants.
- *Defer income taxes.* Any income generated from an annuity is tax deferred, so you pay no taxes on it until you receive a payment from it. And, the longer you keep from withdrawing any funds from the annuity, the more time there will be for the invested funds to produce more gains. This benefit is even greater if you expect to have a lower income tax rate when you retire, in which case any gains paid out after that date will be taxable at the lower rate. This is a major benefit, when you compare an annuity to most other types of investments.
- *Lower your investment risk.* Generally, annuities are not as risky as other types of investment, because they include an insurance component that limits your risk. This results in a more consistent return. This can be of some importance when you are approaching retirement, and want to lock in a reasonable rate of return on your investment.
- *Make larger contributions.* There is no upper cap on the amount of money that you can put into an annuity. This differs from many other tax-deferred accounts, such as IRAs and 401(k) accounts, where there are relatively low caps on contributions.
- *Obtain longer payouts.* An annuity can provide you with a secure series of payments, no matter how long you live. This is an insurance element of an annuity contract.
- *Provide a death benefit.* If you choose this option, many annuity contracts allow you to pay extra for a death benefit that is paid to your beneficiary. While this is not the key reason why people buy annuities, it does represent another advantage of doing so.

Problems with Annuities

Annuities are not a complete panacea, as the preceding section may have implied. There are also several issues with them to be aware of. They are as follows:

- *Complicated rules.* While some annuities have simple rules and are easy to understand, many (such as deferred variable annuity contracts) involve highly complex financial engineering (such as fixed indexed annuities), and incorporate a number of rules regarding when you can access your cash, and in what amounts. It takes a detailed knowledge of annuity contracts to gain a firm understanding of how your annuity contract works.
- *Counterparty risk.* Another issue, which can be characterized as low-probability and high-risk, is that your funds are now in the hands of an insurer, and you are relying on it to stay in business. These entities typically have substantial financial reserves, but it is still possible for them to go bankrupt. If so, you may receive only a fraction of your invested funds back, if any.
- *Delayed payout.* Annuity contracts are commonly used by retirees, who want a long-term income stream and deferred taxable income. The risk they bear is that the annuities may not begin to pay back for a long period of time. This delayed return can present a problem if you are suddenly faced with a liquidity crisis, because the counterparty to your annuity contract has no obligation to return the funds, except in accordance with the payout schedule stated in the agreement.
- *Higher costs.* Annuities can involve fairly large salesperson commissions and other fees. Some contracts even contain clauses that allow the insurer to increase fees in the future. The net result is that a retiree may not experience much of a return on an annuity, despite having made a long series of payments into it. This is a particular concern when you purchase a fixed indexed annuity, because you are paying a commission, plus an options dealer, as well as the manager of any volatility control mechanism applied to the chosen index, plus the insurer. A much cheaper alternative is a no-load mutual fund, but such a fund does not provide the guaranteed payouts that a properly-structured annuity can.
- *Illiquid investments.* Many annuity contracts mandate that you park money in them for an extended period of time, with steep penalties and other restrictions on early withdrawals. This can be a major problem when you have a sudden need for cash, or find another investment that generates a better return.
- *More oversight.* Some contracts involve so many features and trigger dates that you will need to keep track of when certain features are triggered or expire. This may be more investment oversight than you would like.
- *No basis step up with an inherited annuity.* If you receive an annuity through an inheritance, annuity gains are taxed; there is no step-up in basis to the full amount of the inherited funds (which would allow you to avoid paying tax).
- *Taxation at the ordinary income tax rate.* Annuity payouts may be delayed, in which case you can defer paying any related income taxes. However, when

you *do* receive these funds, you will be taxed at the ordinary income tax rate, which will be calculated on the entire payout, if you originally bought the annuity with pre-tax money. If you bought it with after-tax money, then you will only have to pay tax on any gains experienced. Nonetheless, the ordinary income tax rate can be substantial, depending on your income tax bracket.

> **Tip:** Only enter into a contract with an insurer that is rated as excellent, superior, or very good by the rating agencies (such as A.M. Best). A high rating means that a rating agency is of the opinion that the entity has sufficiently strong finances to meet all of its reasonably foreseeable obligations.

When to Invest in an Annuity

Given all of the issues noted in this manual, under what circumstances does it make sense to enter into an annuity contract? This can be a good choice for some, but perhaps not the best for others. Here are several scenarios in which it can make sense:

- *Focus on extra recurring income.* You have a substantial amount of money on hand, and want to convert it into a financial instrument that pays you a recurring amount of money that can supplement your other retirement income. In essence, you want enough extra cash coming in each month to top up your social security payments and allow you to pay for all of your essential expenses.
- *You are likely to live longer.* If you have a healthy lifestyle and come from a family where long lives are the norm, then you may want to acquire an annuity to ensure that you will have a continuing stream of income as you age well into your 90s.
- *You are risk averse.* If you feel that wild swings in the stock market give you nightmares, then consider putting money into an annuity that provides a consistent level of return, or a consistent income stream.
- *You want more tax deferrals.* You may have already maxed out your contributions into other tax-deferred instruments, and want to keep using tax-deferred investments. If so, your ability to tax-defer money in an annuity is essentially unlimited.
- *You want to avoid bank rates of interest.* Banks typically offer low rates of interest on invested funds, including their certificates of deposit. Annuities can typically beat the rates being offered by your bank.

A variation on the question of when to invest in an annuity can be shifted around to *who* should invest in an annuity. The sweet spot is someone with a sufficient amount of cash on hand to pay for an annuity, without being so wealthy that he or she has enough cash available to pay for any type of contingency that may arise. Further, this person should already have maxed out the contributions that can be made to other tax-deferred retirement accounts. Or, numerically, the ideal person who invests in an annuity has extra cash on hand in the general range of $250,000 to $1 million. However, these are general criteria that may not apply to everyone. For example, if someone is at risk of a debilitating illness, it could make sense to obtain an annuity that also provides for nursing home payments.

Another viewpoint on who should invest in annuities is to focus on the stream of income that a person receives. If a person does not have a stable, long-term source of income, then it makes sense to invest in an income annuity during those rare occasions when a large sum of cash is received. For example, if John owns a rental home and pours all rent received back into the unit, then he has very little cash on hand to invest. He then sells the home, clearing $1 million. At this point, he has no ready source of income, and so could elect to invest the money in an income annuity that provides him with an ongoing, reliable source of monthly payments.

Questions to Ask About an Annuity

Many of the concerns raised in this book about annuities can be addressed simply by asking the agent about them while discussing which annuity products would work best for you. Here are some the questions worth raising with the agent:

- What is the guaranteed interest rate, and for how long will it be guaranteed?
- How good is the guaranteed interest rate in comparison to the rates available for other, similar investments?
- Is there a surrender period? If so, how long is it, and what is the surrender charge?
- In case I want to withdraw funds, is there a market value adjustment? If so, how is the adjustment calculated?
- What is the A.M. Best rating for the insurance company?
- What will this contract be worth at the end of the contract period?

Annuity Best Practices

Like any type of investment, there are certain practices that can give you a better return or outcome. Here are several best practices to consider:

- *Avoid surrender charges.* A common complaint about annuities is that your funds are locked up for a long time. There are two ways around this issue. First, only enter into contracts that feature a short surrender period. As another option, maintain a significant pool of cash on the side, to deal with any short-term cash needs that may arise.
- *Choose insurers carefully.* When you are purchasing an income annuity, you are placing a bet that the insurer will remain in business for the rest of your life. If not, your retirement could be destroyed. Consequently, only enter into an income annuity with one of the highest-rated insurers.
- *Convert inherited funds into an annuity.* If you have inherited funds that are in a tax-deferred account, you will need to pay taxes on some or all of these funds. But, if you invest the funds into an income annuity, you only have to

pay income tax when you receive the income. This spreads out the tax payments over many years, which reduces their present value.

- *Examine surrender terms.* Do not purchase a contract that assesses a surrender charge for a longer period than the guaranteed rate of return. In this situation, the insurer could dramatically lower your rate of return after the guarantee period, where you are essentially trapped in the contract because the surrender charge is so high.
- *Shop for quotes.* It is essential to shop for quotes, since the payouts or rates of return offered by various insurers can vary dramatically. If you take the time to obtain a number of quotes, this may result in a substantial improvement in your benefits.
- *Skip contract buyback offers.* If an insurer contacts you and offers to buy back your contract, do not do it. This offer will only be made if the insurer feels that it will generate a profit by taking this step.
- *Switch to life insurance.* If you are quite aged and have enough funds for the remainder of your life, then cash out of your annuity contract, pay taxes on it, and use the residual to buy life insurance on yourself. Your beneficiaries will then have no tax obligation on the insurance payout – which would not be the case if they had instead received your annuity.
- *Wait on an immediate life annuity.* Whenever possible, delay purchasing an immediate life annuity. This annuity begins issuing you a periodic payment as soon as the contract is signed. By waiting until you really need it, you can obtain a larger periodic payment. In addition, by waiting, you are more likely to outlive the other annuity owners in your pool, which entitles you to the survivorship credits from those annuity owners who died before you.

The Money's Worth Ratio

The money's worth ratio (MWR) measures the fairness of the rate of return provided by an insurer under the terms of an annuity contract. It is calculated as the discounted present value of expected future payments, divided by its cost. For example, if you pay an insurer $200,000 for an income annuity that pays out over a 10-year period, this results in a net present value of $185,000, which represents an MWR of 92.5. In essence, you are getting a return of 92.5% of your invested funds.

Any MWR score close to 100 is considered good, while a score closer to 80 indicates that the insurer is likely overcharging you for the benefits that it will provide.

Insurance Company Ratings

As we pointed out earlier in this manual, it is important to only purchase annuities from a financially stable insurer. These parties maintain high levels of liquidity, and so are better able to honor their contractual obligations. The best way to ascertain financial strength is to obtain an insurer's financial strength rating. The ratings are provided by four primary rating agencies, which are A.M. Best, Standard & Poor's, Moody's, and Fitch Ratings. Each of these agencies uses its own rating system to devise a ranking for an insurer. A comparison of their rating systems appears in the following exhibit.

Comparative Insurer Rating Systems

A. M. Best	Standard & Poor's	Moody's	Fitch Ratings
A++	AAA	Aaa	AAA
Superior	Extremely Strong	Exceptional	Exceptionally Strong
A+	AA+	Aa1	AA+
Superior	Very Strong	Excellent	Very Strong
A	AA	Aa2	AA
Excellent	Very Strong	Excellent	Very Strong
A-	AA-	Aa3	AA-
Excellent	Very Strong	Excellent	Very Strong
B++	A+	A1	A+
Good	Strong	Good	Strong
B+	A	A2	A
Good	Strong	Good	Strong
B	A-	A3	A-
Fair	Strong	Good	Strong
B-	BBB+	Baa1	BBB+
Fair	Good	Adequate	Good
C++	BBB	Baa2	BBB
Marginal	Good	Adequate	Good
C+	BBB-	Baa3	BBB-
Marginal	Good	Adequate	Good
C	BB+	Ba1	BB+
Weak	Marginal	Questionable	Moderately Weak
C-	BB	Ba2	BB
Weak	Marginal	Questionable	Moderately Weak
D	BB-	Ba3	BB-
Poor	Marginal	Questionable	Moderately Weak
E	B+	B1	B+
Under Regulatory Supervision	Weak	Poor	Weak
F	B	B2	B
In Liquidation	Weak	Poor	Weak
	B-	B3	B-
	Weak	Poor	Weak
	CCC+	Caa1	CCC+
	Very Weak	Very Poor	Very Weak
	CCC	Caa2	CCC
	Very Weak	Very Poor	Very Weak
	CCC-	Caa3	CCC-
	Very Weak	Very Poor	Very Weak
	CC	Ca	CC
	Extremely Weak	Extremely Poor	Extremely Weak
		C	C
		Lowest	Distressed

A variation on these rating systems is the COMDEX score. This is a composite of the ratings that an insurer has received from the agencies listed in the preceding exhibit.

It provides a rating, on a scale of 1-100, in relation to all other companies that have received ratings.

Note: Though it is generally a good idea to enter into an annuity contract with a top-rated insurer, there are cases in which it can make sense to deal with a lower-rated one. Lower-rated insurers frequently offer higher payout rates than higher-rated insurers, so you might consider one of these contracts when the term is relatively short (such as three years). By entering into a shorter-term contract, you can re-evaluate the insurer at regular intervals, and decide whether you want to continue with them.

Summary

This manual has described the types of annuity contracts in which you can invest, as well as their features, advantages, and disadvantages. It has also covered the tax impact of annuities, the circumstances under which it makes sense to acquire an annuity, and the best practices related to these contracts. By the end of this book, you should have a good idea of whether to invest in an annuity, what type of annuity would work best for you, and which insurers to deal with. The next step is up to you.

Glossary

A

Accumulation phase. The payment phase during which an investment fund is built up.

Annuitant. The party that is entitled to receive annuity payments.

Annuitization phase. The payment phase during which annuity payments are made.

Annuity. A series of fixed payments made at regular intervals.

Annuity owner. The person who signed an annuity contract and pays all premiums.

B

Beneficiary. The person who receives assets when someone else dies.

D

Deferred annuity. A guaranteed lump sum or series of payments, which begin at a point in the future.

F

Fixed annuity. A fixed stream of annuity payments.

I

Immediate annuity. An annuity that provides an immediate guaranteed lifetime payout.

Income annuity. An annuity that generates a stream of income payments that are intended to fund your retirement.

Investment risk. The potential to experience a loss on an investment.

L

Longevity risk. The risk that you will outlive your retirement savings.

N

Non-qualified annuity. An annuity that is acquired with savings on which you have already paid income taxes.

P

Period certain income annuity. An income annuity in which you are only paid for a fixed period of time.

Q

Qualified annuity. An annuity that is purchased with funds that are in a tax-deductible traditional individual retirement account, or an employer-sponsored retirement plan.

R

Reverse mortgage. An annuity product that allows you to borrow against the equity stored up in your home, while still living in it.

S

Surrender period. The amount of time that the owner must wait before withdrawing any funds from an annuity without incurring a penalty.

V

Variable annuity. A stream of payments in which the payments vary based on the success of the underlying investments.

Index

www.ingramcontent.com/pod-product-compliance
Lightning Source LLC
Chambersburg PA
CBHW051431200326
41520CB00023B/7434